ENDVISIBLE

-Hydrus

Published by: Hydrus
Photographs by: Hydrus
Proofreading by: Gabrielle G.
Cover Design by: Cleo Moran - Devoted Pages Designs
Formatting by: Cleo Moran -Devoted Pages Designs
www.devotedpages.com

Manufactured in the United States of America

life lost meaning and gained purpose with one last breath

Dedicated to Mima
3.30.16

Pain sits upon my brow
My strength abundantly distant
Amidst my own treachery
My goal is scarcely persistent

Overcome the sullen odds
Dark pressure that ensues
My silent screams never heard
Inner voices are my muse

Once hope was a beacon
Held tightly within
Judged now and forsaken
Burned for my sins

Judgement
-Hydrus

Vanished from my state
Is the welcoming sound of your voice
Senses without meaning
Longing a simple re-encounter
Yearning for an autumn wind
Only to be left broken again
Lost and forgotten

Abandoned
-Hydrus

Tragic in terms
Words wielded as stones
Thoughts are your enemy
Deeply scorned
Vengeful in thought
Every movement is judged
Emotion uncaged
The true meaning of
Love

Denial
-Hydrus

Moonlight haze
Upon I linger
Twilight naps
A stroking finger

Distant thoughts
I cannot fathom
Memories awake
Dreams so random

Numb to touch
Mind will wander
Feelings are hush
Fear will plunder

Lonely heart
I cannot handle
Silence looms
Upon a mantle

Once again
Endure I will
Nevertheless
My soul lay still

Sleepless
-Hydrus

Eyes open
Images replayed
The night was restless
Emotion overcame

Memories revisited
Sorrow engulfs
Lost sensations
Skin is cold

Reaching to remember
I struggle in vain
Sitting still
Lost in the pain

Thoughts avoided
Will you return
Awaiting the darkness
Memories burn

Visitor
-Hydrus

Shallow empty cruel
Intense
Mangled, burned
Torn
Outstretched

Ripped from within
Abandoned, worn
Emotion
Sore, dim

Revive
Caress
Rebuild
Hope

Still dormant
Dry
Cracked
Life
No more

Discarded
-Hydrus

Piercing blades
Through bone and flesh
Sever
My bleeding soul

Once lit candle
Flare clever and rare
Alone
Truth not told

Lay still
Coldness
No desire
Circumstance
Will unfold

Vacant answers
Will emerge
False Denials
Trials
No one left to hold

Injustice
-Hydrus

The escapades of life
Dwindle on my doorstep
Every moment of my living
Is questioned for my desire to breathe
If only I could find hope
In those things we consider true

Ending
-Hydrus

Alone in my thoughts
Whispers tease and unravel
Feelings unwind
Emotions are gathered

Venom I brew
Mind all a clutter
Twisted thoughts unbound
Silent screams I mutter

Defying to answer
Questions retold
Anger and rage
Truth will be bold

Unwanted confession
Unwavering reason
Forgiveness is lost
Life has no meaning

Betrayed
-Hydrus

Eyes open thoughts of you
Lost emotion
Unseen few

Random thoughts blur my soul
Needing want
Ensnared control

Lost again though light in hand
Excuses of a coward
A tainted stance

One day will I tower
And become a man
Simply to recover
A hopeless path

Mislead
-Hydrus

Quick glance
Silent steps
Creek or crack
You are not there

Distant dream
Echoed voice
Guiding light
You are not there

Nurturing look
Subtle smile
A simple kiss
You are not there

Loving warmth
Unquestionable care
Relentless support
You are not there

Etched words
Deep pain
Endless love
Always there

Etched
-Hydrus

Never could I imagine
Life without you
An empty hand
A world askew

Left alone, abandoned
One can realize
Part of you is gone
Humanity has died

Reality sets in
Habits will reform
Hate lingers inside
Feelings are torn

Everything has changed
Tears start to pour
Aware of the ending
Forever no more

Guilt
-Hydrus

Shadows haunt my dreams
As I lay in the dark
My eyes an empty gaze
That foreshadow all days to come
A dim light glares at me
Through an open door
Behind which awaits haunting nights
And waiting for my fate
With an open heart
False memories of happiness
Are no more

Motionless
-Hydrus

Please let me go
For my soul can't control
The pain that I feel
When you visit me still
I want to hold on
The dreams to be long
You flutter away
Many words left to say

Plead
-Hydrus

A dungeon of sorrows
Chained to my past
Coldness abruptly
Hinders my path

Poisoned and tortured
Rats feast on my soul
Stone cuts at my navel
Death rings to take toll

Screams of an angel
Awaken within
Life no longer
Sons of the sin

Helpless and vacant
My shallow heart insincere
Never repentant
Engulfed in black tears

Light be forgotten
The sun will not rise
End to the rotten
Buried with lies

Gallows
-Hydrus

Rustic vines
Caress my face
As no emotion
Leave a trace

Forgotten whispers
In me laced
Without description
Torn with hate

Can no one hear me
My moans and screams
Nothing beneath me
Unleashed I seem

One day for vengeance
A night of thrill
Never to be forgotten
Again I kill

Caged
-Hydrus

Rain falls from the heavens
As I lay here still in grief
Mourning my lost direction
Waiting for an unexpected thief

One who would steal me
Vanquish my nightmares and misdeeds
Save me from myself
Open the door with the missing key

I await such a splendor
But the silence keeps me ill
My fingertips could render
My life's work I won't fulfill

A burden I must carry
With me the journey slowly fades
The blame is my undoing
My confidence not regained

If only I had answers
Far few the thoughts remain
Sadness engulfs me
All I feel is pain

Helpless
-Hydrus

Yearning your touch
Feeling emotion
Captured your grasp
Weak of devotion

Ripped from clenched fist
Knife wielding gash
Mangled and scorned
Withering past

Fleeing escape
Doom is your spade
Anxious the path
Mirror holds shade

Yells left lonesome
Answers sincere
Vanishing tides
Eclipsing the fear

Reflection
-Hydrus

Lost in my purpose
Trying to find my way
Questions about misfortune
Countless endless days

Yearning for direction
To the sky and stars I gaze
Only to find redemption
My thoughts are in disarray

Hoping for some answers
My soul can only pray
Waiting for this journey
No words to humbly say

Find myself in silence
Running must evade
Failing is my triumph
Confession slowly fades

Deceit
-Hydrus

Days I count
On weathered skin
Til morning rises
You within

Sheets uncover
Contour lines of bliss
Forgotten words
A dark single kiss

Thoughts a hurry
Crowd minds eye
Words are murmured
Endless lies

Yearn for a touch
Skin and bone
Decaying words
Silent groan

Darkness beds
Not to be born
Blood stained passion
Heart is torn

No more desire
Quest less chance
Fading. Fainting
Circumstance

Taken
-Hydrus

Gentle giant
Eyes a glass
Warmth and flurry
Crashing path

Side by side
Grateful journey begins
Thoughts are few
About impending end

Steps are taken
No regard for fate
Friend and son
It's too late

Joy and love
Overflowing bliss
Flight of time
Haltering myth

Never again
to hold your hand

I don't want answers
I will never understand

Suffer
-Hydrus

At my side
never waiver
Unfaltering light
You are my Savior

Moments of loss
Despair and wrath
Judgment not cast
Enlightened path

For You I look
Though in sight remain
Stand alone by choice
Endure all pain

In flesh I bend
Suffering I bleed
Only to be found
Heavenly steed

Lesson not taken
Symptoms recall
You ignore all forsaken
My God, My All

Redemption
-Hydrus

Savage steps
Attract a look
Yearning lips
On the hook

Tempted fate
Drew her in
Hunger came
Hard within

Fingers grab
Pull in close
Flesh aroused
Take in host

Pounding skin
Beating heart
Grinding bones
Naked art

Temptress
-Hydrus

Vanquished loss. Motionless,
dark empty cavern. my heart lay dormant

your will spineless, shattered.
only to realize all is forgiven

Shameless
-Hydrus

Morning rises
Sand dust blooms
Waves are crashing
Fading moon

Footsteps vanish
Wind in hair
Sounds idly dance
Brightly stare

Days upon us
Choices vast
Captured heart
Amidst tall grass

Forever seems endless
Time so few
May the day never end
They always do

Broken Sails
-Hydrus

Joy has left me
Ran off with divine
Left in the shallows
To cry and to whine

Bitter and tortured
Sadness a full
Caged in ones sorrow
The life of a fool

Ridden
-Hydrus

Buried in slumber
Time sits still
Thoughts erratic
Unfulfilled

Sunken in doubt
Darkness descends
No need to run
Can't comprehend

Back at the start
Replaying a scene
Still with emotion
Caught in a dream

Why must it happen
Searching for meaning
Lost without sight
Demons are gleaming

Perched at the beckon
Awaiting a summon
Hands are upon me
Sinfully drunken

Silence engulfs me
No one to aid
Eyes deepen and blacken
Act one quickly fades

Revenant
-Hydrus

Darkened eyes
Questions rise
Why am I here
Feelings inside

Keep the joy
Caged in silent fear
Can't get out
Canceled cheer

Two lives lived
One full of light
Fellow darkness
Full of fright

No one senses
Soul has gone
Lengthy waiting
Strength begone

Wait full scream
Upon thy face
Solemn care
Selfish fate

Yearning changes
None to come
My path once chosen
A life undone

Vanquished
-Hydrus

Casted in chains
Love no desire
Twisted betrayal
A devils choir

Longing for virtue
Seldom found
Slithering bones
Risks all around

Temptation is bliss
Demons below
Venomous kiss
The shriek of a crow

Insult is murder
Impaled by the truth
Witness to vengeance
Hung by the noose

Sentenced
-Hydrus

Is that a flutter
An invitation so bold
A twinkle or blink
Soon turn cold

A spectrum of color
Lavish in depth
Vast as a labyrinth
Moist when wept

Hunted and captured
Lost in it's maze
One only remembers
Evading it's gaze

Prisoner of passion
Suggestions once made
Awareness now gone
Temptation fades

The Encounter
-Hydrus

Still on the surface
Covered in wait
Looking for words
Oddly irate

Hints often few
Just to connect
Senses askew
Much disconnect

One often wonders
Why cry in the dark
A game often played
Two worlds far apart

Victimless crime
Remorseful intent
Feelings of guilt
Wanting to vent

Play the game still
Lead and move on
Smiling afar
Just a come on

Goal is quite simple
Satisfying ones need
To feel true pleasure
Regardless the deed

Left to suffer
An actor mislead
Time to move on
Fantasy dead

Illusions
-Hydrus

Words are so simple
Thrown around to expound
Various feelings
None to be found

Empty intentions
Painted imagery forged
Fables and myths
Letters are gorged

Naive is the reader
Easily wounded
Suffering Joy
Fallen to ground

Real is not so simple
The veil quickly shows
Tales unquestioned
Lies have been sold

Anonymous
-Hydrus

Chances lost
Trial faded
Away from me
Life jaded

Burnt paper
Torn cloth
Jagged edge
Bruised heart

Naked truth
Dry eyes
Swollen chest
Silent cries

Some emotion
Pain is gone
Some commotion
All is wrong

Drowning
-Hydrus

Used for desire
Pride of all scent
Cannot be captured
Guilty lament
Whispers of leather
Moans in the dark
One so clever
Whips make their mark
Grunting silence
Shadows dress flesh
Abundant desires
A slippery sketch
Taste on a finger
Hunger endures
Mounted upon us
Stained tiled floors
Ravish and conjure
A thirst to be quenched
Skin upon skin
Oiled and drenched
Motionless lines
Shattered doors opened wide
Soul has been taken
Nothing to hide

Hidden Pleasure
-Hydrus

Ageless words
Endless time
Lost in you
Eyes are blind

First in all
Never compare
All my passion
So sincere

Betrayed actions
Hidden lust
Shadows abundant
Lost all trust

Ripped wide open
Blood pulled from the womb
Cruel intentions
Darkness looms

Intentions uncovered
Blade in hand
Throat slit open
You don't understand

Never to share
To lose or misplace
Quiet despair
Silent face

Voiceless
-Hydrus

Como los mares de mi alma
Me Deja's con pasión
Deseos y Esperanza
Abrazado a la tentación

Siempre estare a tu lado
Un barco navegado
Contigo en la distancia
Enamorado con toda la confiansa

Hoy sera un nuevo dia
Mi alma como espia
Encontrados y capturando
Mis sueños estrañando

Cadenas
-Hydrus

Souls encounter
Twirling at night
Thinking of you
Heartless sight

Close to my being
Removed from my life
Sharing a canvas
In the twilight

Pretender of hurt
Romantic delight
Urges forgotten
Internal the fight

Savage the ending
Untrue words that lie
All was erased
An instant goodbye

Icarus
-Hydrus

Abandoned wreck
A voyage once kept
Drowning away
As the stars slept

Waves crash on hull
Flightless wet gull
Shattered and torn
Cracked open skull

Moonlight will hide
Many have tried
Tempted by fate
Some often have died

Distant light shine
Mermaids divine
Buried in sand
Treasure less find

Divine Traveler
-Hydrus

A chill runs through me
As I lay on the ground
Lost in love
Not to be found

Hidden fears are rampant
Adorn my view
Silence abundant
Obscures the few

Those who challenge
Wit and braun
Find solace and peace
All is wrong

Judgment, questions
Life not clear
Nomadic moods
Cannot steer

A gamble taken
Hunch, a leap
Lust forsaken
In too deep

Obsession
-Hydrus

Is it true
That moment once held
A catch of an eye
The lips that cast spell

Touch of a finger
Wet mouth so sincere
Innocent glance
Frozen in fear

Love seen so pure
Angelic divine
Twisted and curled
Tangled in vines

Breathe left unspoken
Skin left to hide
Demons awoken
Far reaching cries

Once was a passion
Covered in flies
Heart is now broken
All was a lie

Haunted
-Hydrus

∞

Me hero my champion
My love gone so quick
Courageous in valor
Why you get sick

Fearless and strong
All just went wrong
She was one of a kind
My beautiful Mom

Endless the days
Thoughts are with you
The tears flow daily
My life felt untrue

Far from me you are
A loss way too great
I carry a scar
Till I meet the same fate

I yearn for your arms
Your tight warm embrace
A simple smile
Your beautiful face

Words cannot show
The pain that I feel
I miss you so much
Sometimes I can't deal

Please follow my footsteps
Live in my dreams
Whisper some words
Feelings unseen

You will always be with me
I will always recall
I will love you forever
My Wonderful All

Broken
-Hydrus

Footsteps creep
Along the boards
Senses scream
Silent floors

Raindrops fall
Upon rooftop
Ticking clock
On counter top

Eyes darkened
Linens cool
Foggy whispers
Dormant fool

Jump right up
Ripped from sleep
Heart feels fear
I slowly weep

All alone
Lay awake
Restless time
It's a mistake

Bell rings once
I quickly gasp
Empty words
You have past

The Moment
-Hydrus

Distance kept
Try to be strong
Meaningful silence
Nothings wrong
Away a watcher
Keeps eyes on me
A Vail, a shadow
Secrecy
Every moment
Steps a pace
Looming gestures
Ghostly trace
My breath is silent
Eyes are shut
Hope and pray
A deepened cut
To resume
In stealth I lay
Hunted down
Everyday

Prey
-Hydrus

Winter looms
In the distant days
One only wonders
What will remain
So much lost
No return
A Voyage shattered
All burned
Guided hope
Unspoken deeds
Unravel all created
Left in need
No more chances
Given to us
My life no more
Full of distrust

Scorched
-Hydrus

Buried in thought
Guilt fires my stance
Heavenly rot
A distant romance

A path has been chosen
Unique to the two
So much emotion
Actions are few

Halting all movement
Risk of a fall
Lost in the present
Waiting to call

Each whisper an anchor
Plunging so deep
Temptation no more
The secret you keep

Alone
-Hydrus

Simple addict
Hidden in sight
Play the game
To my delight

Act the master
Rules are set
Turn the tables
My regret

Lose myself
A maze redrawn
Running scared
I am the pawn

What was started
With no end
Hollow feelings
One not pretend

Dangerous game
Crying in distress
Lesson not learned
I must confess

Labyrinth
-Hydrus

Life of another
Behind walls
all is clear

Words cloud the truth
To hide
Disappear

Uncovering feeling
Once jaded
Now seen

Unfairly forgotten
Cruelty
A dream

Alone
Defiant
Broken
Yell scream

Without you
Forgiveness
No more
To be seen

Condemned
-Hydrus

Wandering stare
Words caress
Yearning skin
Morning undress

Figure in water
Outlined in mist
Wishful desires
Stolen glimpse

Drop painted flesh
Fingers will chase
Tempestuous form
Lips will retrace

Rendezvous
-Hydrus

Subtle smile glistens
Eyes shimmer through glass
Strands of hair cover
Distant dark past

How life has forgotten
Through moons and rise failed
Streaming tears over cheek
Heart is impaled

Through virtue of might
Strength of ones sin
Lost souls are recovered
The future still dim

Hope is a wanderer
Far away are it's moans
Always an onlooker
Desperate groans

Fate has befallen
Triumphant death waits
Shadows upon me
No more escape

Specter
-Hydrus

Grateful to breathe
Live amongst the trees
Hold you in my hands
Always understand
You will be in my life
Forever never thinking twice
My Guardian to the End
Who I will always defend
Protector of my mind
Your scriptures will define
The Person I must be
All live within me

Bliss
-Hydrus

Quiet laughs
Inner thoughts
Stumbling through
A familiar corpse
Seen this movie once before
I've played the role
You so adore
My turn comes
To play the fool
No advice
Life's so cruel

The Fool
-Hydrus

Ocean engulf me
To the sea I entrust thee
Wash over my fear
The water grows near

Life will no longer
My soul left to plunder
Lost with no hunger
Thirsting to be

Cowardly plot
Flesh washed upon rock
Always forgotten
Heart left to rot

Solace
-Hydrus

Tender glances on sheets so white
Whispering doodles in your delight
Pensive moments words unveil
Strokes of color your breath exhale
Endless thoughts and words in stream
Expressions of an innocent dream
Capture time with every line
Framed in Love that's so divine

Essence
-Hydrus

Never to be
Life seldomly
Reminds us to see
One triumphantly

Losses abundant
Choices reluctant
Misfortune a constant
Image repugnant

Dire the motive
Inside so corroded
Feelings eroded
Esteem imploded

Soulless for seeking
Answers not pleasing
Silence the speaking
Embrace the sleeping

Our doubt is relentless
Sadness a temptress
I quietly undress
The voices can now rest

Buried
-Hydrus

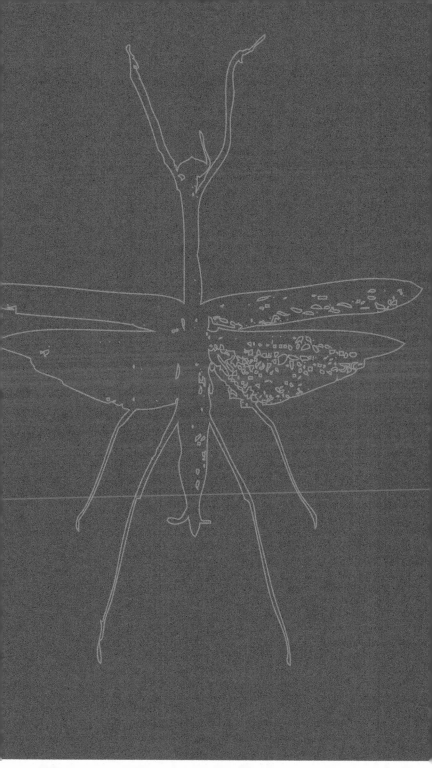

To all my loved ones
who shaped my journey.

C./G.

Thank you.

"Words have no power to impress
the mind without the exquisite
horror of their reality. "

Edgar Allan Poe

About The Author

Hydrus is an anonymous poet, photographer,
and artist.

His belief is that one has never really
found their true self until
they have understood and conquered
their darkest demons.

His poems are meant to illustrate an
individual struggle while
navigating through life and all of its
unforeseen obstacles.

Connect with hydrus:

Instagram: instagram.com/hydruspoetry

Made in the USA
Las Vegas, NV
10 March 2021